Ginn

Social Studies

All About Rules

Authors

Jane Milliken

Arlene Tanz

Consultants

Dawn Hastings

Adele Owatz

Donna Panasis

Margaret Ryall

Nancy Thomas

Dianne Wilkins

Ginn

Toronto

We all follow rules.
Rules keep us safe and make our lives better.
Every family has rules.

What rules does this family have?

Draw 3 rules that you have at home.
Ask an older person what rules they
had when they were children.

There are rules at school.

What are the rules here?
Who is following them?
Who is breaking them?

Write or draw a
classroom rule.

There are rules in the community.

What rules do you see here?

Choose a rule.
Pretend to follow it.
Pretend to break it.

There are special rules for special places.

What can you tell about the rules here?

No Running on Deck
No Diving

 Make signs to help you remember a rule.

We all have responsibilities.
We help in our community.

How are these people helping?

Choose someone on the page.
Role-play how that person helps.
Share your role-play with the class.

We all have rights.
We all need to be treated fairly.

How are these people treating one another?

 Make a poster, book, video, or play to show children's rights.

Every person in a family has rights.
Every person in a family has responsibilities.

Make a poster to show family rights and responsibilities.

Look Back

Look back at your book.
Find someone who follows each of the rules
shown below.